THE
DREAM
JOURNAL

For my sweet friend Nina ♡
keep dreaming
keep writing
keep loving

I love you
XOX ♡ Marian
April 28, '89

Nothing so much convinces me of the boundlessness of the human mind as its operations in dreaming.

—WILLIAM BENTON CLULOW
(1802–1882)
English clergyman

How my quiet thoughts
wander
—beyond the boundless
shores.

—TAO CHI
(1641–c. 1710)
Chinese painter, poet, and scholar

We are asleep with
compasses in our hands.

—W.S. MERWIN
b. 1927
American poet

Take, if you must, this
little bag of dreams,
Unloose the cord, and they
will wrap you round.
—WILLIAM BUTLER YEATS
(1865–1939)
Irish poet

Dreams are our truest friends: they entertain us, they encourage us, they educate us, they soothe us, and most importantly they free us.

—BILL BEHAM
b. 1955
American entrepreneur

One of the most adventurous things left us is to go to bed. For no one can lay a hand on our dreams.

—E. V. LUCAS
(1868–1938)
English novelist and poet

If you can remember dreams of flying and soaring like a bird, or dancing, or singing more perfectly than you ever thought possible, you know that no second-hand account of such events could ever give you the thrill you felt in the dream.

—GAYLE DELANEY
Twentieth-century American psychologist and writer

It is only through a
dream that you can
measure the force of your
love and pain.

—OLGA ILYIN
b. 1900?
Russian-born American writer

That we are not much sicker and much madder than we are is due exclusively to the most blessed and blessing of all natural graces, sleep.

—ALDOUS HUXLEY
(1894–1963)
English writer

Dreaming permits each
and every one of us to be
quietly and safely insane
every night of our lives.

—WILLIAM DEMENT
 b. 1928
 American psychiatrist

The pleasure of the true dreamer does not lie in the substance of the dream, but in this: that there things happen without any interference from his side, and altogether outside his control.

—ISAK DINESEN
(1885–1962)
Danish writer

We sometimes from
dreams pick up some hint
worth improving
by. . .reflection.

—THOMAS JEFFERSON
(1743–1826)
Third U.S. President

Life is a ticklish
business; I have resolved
to spend it in reflecting
upon it.

—ARTHUR SCHOPENHAUER
(1788–1860)
German philosopher

A moment's insight is sometimes worth a life's experience.

—OLIVER WENDELL HOLMES
(1809–1894)
American physician and writer

It is better not to reflect
at all than not to reflect
enough.

—TRISTAN BERNARD
(1866–1947)
French writer

Almost suspended, we
are laid asleep
In body, and become a
living soul:
While with an eye made
quiet by the power
Of harmony, and the deep
power of joy,
We see into the life of
things.

—WILLIAM WORDSWORTH
(1770–1850)
English poet

Vision is the art of
seeing things invisible.
—JONATHAN SWIFT
(1667–1745)
British writer

Nothing is lost on him
who sees.

—THOMAS MOORE
(1779–1852)
Irish poet

What is essential is invisible to the eye.

—ANTOINE DE SAINT-EXUPERY
(1900–1944)
French aviator and writer

We see sleeping what
we wish for waking.

—GEORGE PETTIE
(1548–1589)
English writer

All the things one has forgotten scream for help in dreams.

—ELIAS CANETTI
b. 1905
Bulgarian-born English writer

How odd is the world of dreams! Thoughts, inner speech crowd and swarm—a little world hastening to live before the awakening that is its end, its particular death.

—JULES RENARD
(1864–1910)
French writer

Was it a vision, or a waking dream? Fled is that music:—Do I wake or sleep?

—JOHN KEATS
(1795–1821)
British poet

The first moment of wakefulness is a moment of truth...

—SAMUEL SHEM
Twentieth-century American novelist

We sometimes congratulate ourselves at the moment of waking from a troubled dream: it may be so the moment after death.

—NATHANIEL HAWTHORNE
(1804–1864)
American novelist

For if a man should
dream of heaven and,
waking, find within his hand
a flower as token that he
had really been there—
what then, what then?

—THOMAS WOLFE
  (1900–1938)
  American writer

Men have conceived a twofold use of sleep: that it is a refreshing of the body in this life; that it is a preparing of the soul for the next.

—JOHN DONNE
(1573–1631)
English poet

We often forget our dreams so speedily: if we cannot catch them as they are passing out the door, we never set eyes on them again.

—WILLIAM HAZLITT
(1778–1830)
English writer

Put all that truth down
so you never lose it.

—JAMES GRADY
b. 1949
American writer

I should have lost many a good hit, had I not set down at once things that occurred to me in my dreams.

—SIR WALTER SCOTT
(1771–1832)
Scottish writer

The dream does not end
when we wake up and write
it down.

—MARK A. THURSTON
*Twentieth-century American
psychologist and writer*

Nothing can be
brought to an end in the
unconscious; nothing is past
or forgotten.

—SIGMUND FREUD
(1856–1939)
Austrian psychoanalyst

A dream is the theater where the dreamer is at once scene, actor, prompter, stage manager, author, audience and critic.

—CARL G. JUNG
    (1875–1961)
    Swiss psychiatrist

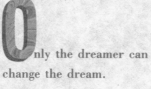

Only the dreamer can change the dream.

—JOHN LOGAN
(1748–1788)
Scottish clergyman and poet

One of the
characteristics of the dream
is that nothing surprises us
in it.

—JEAN COCTEAU
 (1889–1963)
 French writer and film director

In dreams we see
ourselves naked and acting
out real characters, even
more clearly than we see
others awake.

—HENRY DAVID THOREAU
  (1817–1862)
  American writer

Sleep is often the only occasion in which man cannot silence his conscience; but the tragedy of it is that when we do hear our conscience speak in sleep, we cannot act, and that, when able to act, we forget what we knew in our dream.

—ERICH FROMM
(1900–1980)
American psychoanalyst

Within each one of us
there is another whom we
do not know. He speaks to
us in dreams and tells us
how differently *he* sees us
from how *we* see ourselves.

—CARL G. JUNG
(1875–1961)
Swiss psychiatrist

I do not know whether I was then a man dreaming I was a butterfly, or whether I am now a butterfly dreaming I am a man.

—CHUANG TZU
(369–286 B.C.)
Chinese philosopher and teacher

Sometimes I feel like a figment of my own imagination.

—LILY TOMLIN
b. 1939
American actress and comedienne

To me dreams are part of nature, which harbours no intention to deceive but expresses something as best it can...

—CARL G. JUNG
(1875–1961)
Swiss psychiatrist

The dream-work...does not think, calculate, or judge in any way at all; it restricts itself to giving things a new form.

—SIGMUND FREUD
(1856–1939)
Austrian psychoanalyst

Dreams full oft are found of real events the forms and shadows.

—JOANNA BAILLIE
(1762–1851)
Scottish writer

It is a common
experience that a problem
difficult at night is resolved
in the morning after the
committee of sleep has
worked on it.

—JOHN STEINBECK
(1902–1968)
American writer

Have you ever slept on a problem and awakened the next morning with the solution? Elias Howe did, and he invented the popular sewing machine; Igor Stravinsky did, and he created 'The Rite of Spring'...

—GAYLE DELANEY
Twentieth-century American psychologist and writer

A dream itself is but a shadow.

—WILLIAM SHAKESPEARE
(1564–1616)
English playwright

h
...**h**ow light

Must dreams themselves be;

seeing they're more slight

Than the mere nothing that

engenders them!

—JOHN KEATS

(1795–1821)

British poet

We grow great by dreams. All big men are dreamers. They see things in the soft haze of a spring day or in the red fire of a long winter's evening.

—WOODROW WILSON
(1856–1924)
28th U.S. President

Nothing goes unseen
but that which has no place
in the beholder.

—LESLIE JEANNE SAHLER
b. 1952
American writer

As dreams are the fancies of those that sleep, so fancies are but the dreams of those awake.

—SIR THOMAS POPE BLOUNT
(1649–1697)
English writer

I am indeed a practical
dreamer. . . I want to
convert my dreams into
realities as far as possible.

—MAHANDAS GANDHI
(1869–1948)
Hindu statesman

Those who dream by day are cognizant of many things which escape those who dream only by night.

—EDGAR ALLEN POE
(1809–1849)
American writer

Men never cling to
their dreams with such
tenacity as at the moment
when they are losing faith
in them, and know it, but
do not dare to confess it to
themselves.

—WILLIAM GRAHAM SUMNER
(1840–1910)
American economist

More people are
afraid of their dreams than
their nightmares.

—JAMES GRADY
  b. 1949
  American writer

Let not our babbling
dreams affright our souls.

—WILLIAM SHAKESPEARE
(1564–1616)
English playwright

I believe that dreams transport us through the underside of our days, and that if we wish to become acquainted with the dark side of what we are, the signposts are there, waiting for us to translate them.

—GAIL GODWIN
b. 1937
American writer

The greatest act of faith that a man can perform is the act that we perform every night. We abandon our identity, we turn our soul and body into chaos and old night.

—G.K. CHESTERTON
(1874–1936)
English writer

...**r**elaxing into sleep
took the same kind of
courage that jumping out of
a space ship into the
empty...expanse of the
dark universe required.

—NANCY THAYER

b. 1943
American writer

When my soul wearies
of humanity,
when my eyes tire of
staring into the face of
the day,
I wander where the
phantoms of past ages
sleep.

—KAHLIL GIBRAN
(1883–1931)
Syrian writer and artist

O that our dreamings
   all of sleep or wake
Would all their colors from
   the sunset take:
From something of material
   sublime,
Rather than shadow our own
   Soul's daytime
In the dark void of night.

—JOHN KEATS
(1795–1821)
British poet

A lost but happy dream may shed its light upon our waking hours, and the whole day be infected with the gloom of a dreary or sorrowful one; yet of neither may we be able to recover a trace.

—WALTER JOHN DE LA MARE
(1873–1956)
English writer

If I awake surrounded by flowers, I can hardly remember my sad dreams.

—TRADITIONAL SPANISH SONG

There was a time when
   meadow, grove, and stream
The earth, and every
   common sight,
To me did seem
Apparelled in celestial light,
The glory and the freshness
   of a dream.
—WILLIAM WORDSWORTH
(1770–1850)
British poet

There is a prodigious
selfishness in dreams: they
live perfectly deaf and
invulnerable amid the cries
of the real world.

—GEORGE SANTAYANA
(1863–1952)
*Spanish-born American poet and
philosopher*

For to dream and then to return to reality only means that our qualms suffer a change of place and significance.

—COLETTE
(1873–1954)
French writer

I am interested in the effect dreams may have upon our lives. I do not care much about what my living does to my dreams, but I would like to know how my dreaming shapes (if it does) my life.

—JESSAMYN WEST
(1907–1984)
American writer

It is easy to forget that it was dreams that led you to where you are now.

—BILL BEHAM, b. 1955
American entrepreneur

Nothing said to us, nothing we can learn from others, reaches us so deep as that which we find in ourselves.

—THEODORE REIK
(1888–1969)
Austrian-born American psychiatrist

We need time to dream, time to remember, and time to reach the infinite. Time to be.

—GLADYS TABER
(1899–1980)
American writer

Myths are public
dreams, dreams are private
myths.

—JOSEPH CAMPBELL
(1903–1987)
American mythologist and writer

The waking have one world in common; sleepers have each a private world of his own.

—HERACLITUS
(c. 600-500 B.C.)
Greek philosopher

Dreams have only one owner at a time. That's why dreamers are lonely.

—ERMA BOMBECK
b. 1927
American writer and humorist

Children love to be alone because alone is where they know themselves, and where they dream.

—ROGER ROSENBLATT
b. 1940
American writer

Since we are destined
to live out our lives in the
prison of our minds, our
one duty is to furnish it
well.

—PETER USTINOV
b. 1921
English actor and author

It is at night . . . that the mind is most clear, that we are most able to hold all our life in the palm of our skull.

—BRIAN ALDISS
b. 1925
English writer and critic

Nowhere can man find
a quieter or more untroubled
retreat than in his own soul.

—MARCUS AURELIUS
(121-180)
Roman emperor and philosopher

Even sleepers are
workers and collaborators
in what goes on in the
universe.

—HERACLITUS
(c. 600-500 B.C.)
Greek philosopher

If the dream is a translation of waking life, waking life is also a translation of the dream.

—RENÉ MAGRITTE
(1898-1967)
Belgian artist

...**O**nce in a dream somewhere, sometime, somespace, they had managed for a moment to touch another human soul and understand it.

—JAMES JONES
(1921-1977)
American novelist

All dreams of the soul
End in a beautiful man's or
woman's body.

—WILLIAM BUTLER YEATS
(1865-1939)
Irish writer

The net of the sleeper catches fish.

—GREEK PROVERB

Dreams say what they
mean, but they don't say it
in daytime language.

—GAIL GODWIN
b. 1937
American writer

Dreams are faithful interpreters of our inclinations; but there is an art required to sort and understand them.

—MONTAIGNE
(1533-1592)
French writer

Many's the long night
I've dreamed of cheese—
toasted, mostly.

—ROBERT LOUIS STEVENSON
(1850-1894)
Scottish writer

It takes a lot of courage
to show your dreams to
someone else.

—ERMA BOMBECK
b. 1927
American writer and humorist

Don't tell me what you dream'd last night, for I've been reading Freud.

—FRANKLIN PIERCE ADAMS
(1881-1960)
American writer

Seven hundred years
ago...people took dreams
as seriously as the
psychiatrists do today.
—T.H. WHITE
(1906-1964)
English writer

He who would inter-
pret a dream must himself
be, so to speak, on a level
with the dream, for in no
single thing can one ever
hope to see beyond what
one is oneself.

—CARL G. JUNG
  (1875-1961)
  Swiss psychiatrist

A dream which is not understood is like a letter which is not opened.
—*THE TALMUD*

...**m**any times the
message of a dream is not
hidden.

—MARK A. THURSTON
*Twentieth-century American
psychologist and writer*

In sleep we receive confirmation—I cannot find another more fitting word. We receive confirmation that we must go on living.

—ANDREI SINYAVKSY
b. 1925
Russian-born French writer

Existence would be
intolerable if we were never
to dream.

—ANATOLE FRANCE
(1844-1924)
French writer

Dreams take us to levels that we would otherwise be afraid to strive for.

—BILL BEHAM
b. 1955
American entrepreneur

Reality always
lies beyond...
—JOHN BERGER
b. 1926
British writer and art critic